ULURU-KATA TJUTA TRAVEL GUIDE 2024

The Ultimate Uluru (Ayers Rock) Kata Tjuta (The Olgas) Guide: Uncover Ancient Wonders, Mystical Landscape, Indigenous Stories and Unforgettable Adventures in this Majestic Red Heart of Australia For First Timers

ANDREW NICHOLAS

Copyright © [ANDREW NICHOLAS] [2023]

All rights reserved. No part of this publication may be reproduced, distributed or transmitted in any form or by any electronic or mechanical means including information storage and retrieval systems without permission in writing from the publisher, except by a reviewer who may quote brief passages in a review

Table of Contents

Introduction
History of Uluru-kata Tjuta
Cultural Significance
Geology

Chapter 1: Planning Your Trip
Best Time to Visit
Travel Preparation and Packing
Traveling on a Budget
Why Visit Uluru-Kata Tjuta?

Chapter 2: Top Tourist Attractions in Uluru-Kata Tjuta
Uluru (Ayers Rock)
Kata Tjuta (The Olgas)
Walpa Gorge
Mutitjulu Waterhole
Aboriginal Cultural Center
Sunset and Sunrise Viewing Points
Valley of the Winds
Mount Conner
Kings Canyon
The Majestic Monolith

Maruku Arts and Crafts

Chapter 3: Best Transportation Options
Getting to Uluru-Kata Tjuta
Getting Around Uluru-Kata Tjuta

Chapter 4: Best Accommodation Guide
Types of Accommodations
Where to Stay in Uluru-Kata Tjuta
Things to do in Uluru

Chapter 5: Culinary Delights, Regional Specialties, and Restaurants
Local cuisines
Restaurants, Bars and Cafes
Pubs in Uluru

Chapter 6: Uluru-Kata Tjuta's Cultural and Natural History
The Anangu People and Culture
Geological History

Flora and Fauna
Watarrka National Park

Chapter 7: Outdoor Activities in Uluru-Kata Tjuta
Hiking in Uluru-Kata Tjuta
Camel Tours
Helicopter Tours
Stargazing
Photography
Birdwatching
Aboriginal Guided Tours

Chapter 8: Uluru's Art and Cultural Scene
Art galleries and Museums
Festivals and Events
Wildlife
Nightlife

Chapter 9: Practical Tips for Traveling in Uluru-Kata Tjuta
Respect for Indigenous Culture
Language And Useful Phrases
Safety and Health
Shopping for Souvenirs

Custom Etiquette
Traveling with Children

Conclusion
Encouragement Quotes
Useful Websites and Resources

Uluru–kata Tjuta

Introduction

Discover the enigmatic landscapes and ancient treasures of Australia's red heart, Uluru-Kata Tjuta. The remarkable stories concealed within the famous Uluru (Ayers Rock) and Kata Tjuta (The Olgas) can be unearthed with the help of this comprehensive tour guide.

Expect to be enthralled by the Red Centre's attraction as you set out on this adventure; it's a region rich in cultural significance and breathtakingly beautiful. Encountering Uluru and Kata Tjuta's magic will undoubtedly leave an enduring impression on your spirit, regardless of your level of travel experience.

The secrets woven into the very fabric of this ancient country will be revealed as we explore Uluru-kata Tjuta's rich history and trace the footsteps of time. Every chapter relates a story that has influenced the Red Heart's cultural fabric, from the indigenous protectors of the area to the pioneers who saw these amazing formations for the first time.

We investigate the geology and mythology that shape Uluru and Kata Tjuta, going beyond what is seen. Glimmer in the tales and legends that have been passed down through the ages, and marvel at the geological grandeur that bear witness to millions of years of natural sculpting. These Dreamtime-inspired stories combine the spiritual and material worlds, providing a strong bond with the land.

We'll walk you through the Ultimate Uluru-Kata Tjuta experience, so prepare ready for an incredible journey. This book is your ticket to a trip that goes beyond time and space in the center of Australia, from the breathtaking sunrises and sunsets that fill the sky with vivid colors to the wind carrying the echoes of old tales.

History of Uluru-Kata Tjuta

Located in Australia's Northern Territory, Uluru-kata Tjuṯa National Park is a protected area. Kata Tjuta and Uluru are located in the park. It is 440 kilometers (270 mi) south-west of Alice Springs via the Stuart and Lasseter Highways, and 1,943 kilometers (1,207 mi) south of Darwin via road. The landmarks that give the park its name—Uluru and Kata Tjuta, located 40 kilometers (25 mi) to the west—are included in its 1,326 square kilometer (512 sq mi) area. Its natural and cultural landscape has earned it a UNESCO World Heritage Site designation.

For thousands of years, Uluru-Kata Tjuta has been a marvel of geology and culture. An intricate web of tales and meaning is woven together by the rich history of this landmark location and the ancient Indigenous roots.

These enormous sandstone formations are the first reminder of Uluru's geological past. During the Alice Springs Orogeny, about 500 million years ago, Uluru and Kata Tjuta were formed. This monolithic structure was created by processes of sedimentation and uplift. Iron oxidation gives this area its distinct red tint, which adds to its mystique.

It is well known that Uluru appears to change color throughout the day and year, especially at sunrise and sunset when it glows red. Sandstone contains iron oxide, which gives the rock its reddish hue.

Len Tuit, a resident of Alice Springs, escorted a group of schoolboys on a tour to Uluru in 1950, the same year that Ayers Rock National Park was officially recognized. He saw the rock's immense tourism potential and started conducting regular excursions in 1955, bringing drinking water from Curtin Springs and camping for visitors. Ayers Rock-Mount Olga National Park was established in 1958 with the inclusion of Kata Tjuta. The same year, a new airfield opened, enabling the first fly-in, fly-out tour groups in addition to the construction of the first permanent lodging.

On the other hand, the Anangu people, the land's traditional proprietors, have a strong cultural connection to Uluru-Kata Tjuta and its genuine history. Stories of creation and ancestors have been told in this area for many years, making it a spiritual and sacred place. According to Anangu belief, the rock formations are tangible proof of the travels and activities of their ancestors during the Tjukurpa (Dreamtime).

With the advent of explorers and settlers into the interior of Australia in the late 19th century, European exploration and contact with Uluru-Kata Tjuta began. In the 1870s, a European made the first known sighting. The Chief Secretary of South Australia, Sir Henry Ayers, is the reason why surveyor

William Christie Gosse gave the rock its name. When Uluru became known outside of the indigenous communities, this signaled the start of a new chapter in the monument's history.

The Anangu people were to regain official possession of Uluru-Kata Tjuta, nevertheless, only in the later half of the 20th century, when the Australian government recognized the need of managing, protecting, and honoring this holy site's cultural patrimony

Further highlighting Uluru-Kata Tjuta's significance on a global scale was its 1987 UNESCO World Heritage status, which acknowledged the site's cultural and spiritual value in addition to its natural wonders. Discover the history carved into the old rock formations, hear the

Dreamtime stories passed down through the years, and observe the careful balancing act between preservation and tourism in this sacred region when you visit this spectacular red heart of Australia today.

Cultural Significance

Since the Anangu people are the original guardians of this holy site, Uluru-Kata Tjuta has great cultural value derived from their customs and beliefs. Massive sandstone formations that represent a close bond between the land and its people, these sites have been Anangu people's spiritual and cultural center for many years.

The spiritual Dreamtime, or Tjukurpa, is deeply ingrained in the culture. It tells tales of creation, ancestors, and the natural world as it meanders over the countryside.

The elaborate rock formations of Kata Tjuta are home to stories about the creation and travels of the Tjukuritja, (ancestors), who are thought to reside in Uluru.

In the eyes of the Anangu people, Uluru and Kata Tjuta are living archives of cultural knowledge and wisdom, not just physical landmarks. Throughout the ages, stories and rituals have been conveyed through the artwork carved into the rock formations. This visual chronicle that these representations provide for both current and future generations preserves the rich fabric of Anangu culture.

Anangu traditional rites and rituals rely heavily on the sacred grounds surrounding Uluru-Kata Tjuta. Since these locations are not just breathtaking geological formations but also hallowed places where the spirit and essence of the Tjukurpa are strongly sensed, visitors are frequently advised to respect the cultural sensitivities attached to certain spots.

Apart from the physical terrain, the cultural significance also includes ancestor spirits, the Anangu people's ongoing cultural rituals, and the interconnectivity of the natural world. Discovering Uluru-Kata Tjuta allows visitors to go beyond the surface and into the very soul of the land and its people. This experience immerses them in the profound spirituality and cultural richness that permeate this majestic red heart of Australia.

Geology

The word "inselberg" refers to Uluru, a "island mountain". A notable, isolated remaining knob or hill in a hot, dry area that rises sharply from broad, generally level erosion plains around it is called an inselberg. The name "monolith" is also frequently applied to Uluru, however geologists normally steer clear of this dubious phrase.

Uluru's unique quality is its homogeneity, which prevents soil and scree slopes from developing at bedding surfaces by not joining or splitting. It survived when the nearby rocks were being eroded because of these qualities.

Geologists call the rock strata that make up Uluru the Mutitjulu Arkose, and they are one of the many sedimentary formations that fill the Amadeus Basin, in order to record and describe the region's geological history.

Chapter 1

Planning Your Trip

Best Time to Visit

Generally speaking, May through September are the ideal months to visit Uluru-Kata Tjuta National Park, as these months have the highest daytime temperatures of 20°C to 30°C. Warm, but not oppressively so, the days are dry. Though you'll need to be ready for hot, muggy weather, summer travels are still possible. Rain or shine, Uluru is majestic regardless of the season; the kind of experience you seek will ultimately determine when to visit.

Located in the heart of the Outback, you might assume Uluru-Kata Tjuta National Park is hot and dry all year round. But it's quite the opposite! There can be harsh weather in this semi-arid desert region. In contrast to winter, which is warm and dry during the day and frequently experiences below-freezing temperatures at night, summer is oppressive and occasionally stormy (the amount of precipitation varies from year to year).

For your convenience, we have categorized each season.

Spring (September - November)
As the desert comes to life, welcome the blooming flora. Comfortable hiking conditions are provided by mild temperatures.

Summer (December - February)

Discover the landscape's vivid hues beneath Australia's scorching sun. Nevertheless, this is not the best time to see Uluru. During the day, it may get quite hot and humid, with most days falling into the mid-30s. Only in the shadow did the highest temperature ever recorded reach a peak of 45.5 Celsius! We suggest attempting a different time of year unless you enjoy perspiring like a pig. Especially in December and January, be ready for high temperatures.

Autumn (March - May)
Take advantage of the lovely weather and admire the breathtaking sunsets that this season has to offer. Excellent for people who want less crowds and cooler weather.

Winter (June - August)
Feel the chillier air, especially in the evening. Ideal for stargazing, the pure skies

bring out the beauties of the Southern Hemisphere's night sky. Travelers are most active during this time of year, especially those from the US and Europe. During this time, there is always a greater chance of seeing the magnificent Uluru and best deals on travel, lodging, tours, and other activities. Try visiting during Australian holiday times instead of those in Europe or America if you want to avoid the crowds.

Which time of day is optimal?
Daytime

Daytime travel is equally as exciting if you want to get your beauty sleep. The optimum time to visit will depend on the month you go, either in the morning or the afternoon. We advise taking a guided tour to see the site during prime time, when it's most photogenic for Instagram-worthy shots!

Sunset and Sunrise

Famous for its magnificent vistas at sunrise and sunset, Uluru is a must-see location. This is where you may witness the rock's color change in real time. The atmosphere's water vapor and dust particles function as a filter to exclude blue light from incoming solar radiation, giving rise to the enhancing colors. This lets the red light shine through, bouncing off the clouds, the rock, and the surroundings to create a stunningly vibrant display of color. Traveling early in the morning or exploring late at night is well worth it.

Uluru Climate And Five Seasons

Rainfall averages 284.6 mm (11.2 in) annually in the harsh desert climate of the park. Winter (June–August) average low temperature is 4.7 °C (40.5 °F), while summer (December–February) average high temperature is 37.8 °C (100.0 °F). The park has experienced severe temperature readings of 5 °C (23 °F) in the winter and 46 °C (115 °F) in the summer. Between October and March, the UV index shows extremely high UV levels, averaging between 11 and 15.

Indigenous inhabitants (Aboriginals) in the area identify five seasons:

Tjuntalpa: (April/May) – Clouds roll in from the south
Wari: (June/July) – Cold season bringing morning frosts
Piriyakutu: (August/September/October) – Animals breed and food plants flower
Mai Wiyaringkupai: (November/December) – The hot season when food becomes scarce

Itjanu: (January/February) – Sporadic storms can roll in suddenly

Wanitjunkupai (March): Getting chilly

Tjuntalpa (April/May): The south brings in clouds.

Wari (June/July): Morning frosts are a feature of the cold season.

Piriyakutu (August/September/ October): Animals reproduce, and food plants bloom.

Mai Wiyaringkupai (November/ December): The hot season when food is in short supply and scarce.

Itjanu (January/February): Sporadic storms have the potential to arrive suddenly.

Travel Preparation and Parking

Traveling to Uluru-Kata Tjuta National Park necessitates careful preparation and compliance with standard travel regulations. Being well-prepared and aware of the requirements for visiting this famous red heart of Australia are the first steps towards guaranteeing a flawless encounter.

1. Visa and Permits:
Verify your Australia visa needs before visiting this captivating country. Make sure your visa is still valid for the whole time you plan to visit. A separate permit, which may be obtained online or at the park's entry station, is also necessary for visitors visiting Uluru-Kata Tjuta National Park.

2. Packing Essentials:
Travel small, but don't overlook the necessities. Sunglasses, a hat, layered clothes, and sturdy walking shoes. Protect yourself from the harsh Australian sun with a high SPF sunscreen. Sunscreen-protected

lip balm to avoid drying out. A portable shade umbrella for when you need a rest. It's important to be ready for temperature changes, particularly when going on trips at sunrise and sunset.

3. Hydration Essentials and First Aid Kit: A reusable water bottle to keep hydrated in the dry weather, is electrolyte sachets to restore minerals lost during perspiration. Hydration pack for hiking that allows hands-free access to water. Basic medical supplies: bandages, analgesics, and any prescription drugs that you may have. To keep mosquitoes and flies away, use insect repellent.

Put your health first by familiarizing yourself with local health advisories and recommended vaccines.

4. Booking Accommodations:

Make sure to reserve your lodging well in advance, particularly during popular times of the year. Making reservations in advance guarantees a comfortable stay amidst the breathtaking surroundings, whether you decide on a posh resort or go camping.

5. Transportation:

Make sensible plans for your inside-the-park mobility. For greater flexibility, even though shuttle services are offered, think about hiring a car. If you intend to visit some of the park's less accessible parts, be sure your car is equipped for off-road driving.

6. Photography Gear and Navigation tool:

A quality camera or smartphone with adequate capacity for capturing magnificent scenery. Spare memory cards and batteries for prolonged photo sessions. A reliable map or GPS gadget for traversing the wide expanses of the region. Binoculars for spotting wildlife and distant rock formations.

Camping gear (if applicable): Lightweight and compact tent for camping under the stars. Sleeping bag suited for the projected temperature range. Portable camping stove and equipment for preparing meals.

7. Hiking socks and Quick-dry towel
If you're piling up the kilometres, it's worth buying a few pairs of quality hiking socks. They make all the difference as they're designed to keep your feet dry and avoid blisters. Quick-dry towels are wonderful for camping as they roll up compact in your bag and they dry, well, pretty quick. They

also double up as a beach towel, which is handy to carry to waterholes.

8. Respect for Indigenous Culture:
For a greater understanding of the indigenous culture and history, familiarize yourself with the Anangu people. Respect the cultural value of the land by following their norms and guidelines. Avoid climbing Uluru, as it goes against the intentions of the Anangu people, the traditional owners of the land.

9. Environmental Awareness:
Reduce the amount of damage you cause to the environment by practicing responsible tourism. Uluru-Kata Tjuta's natural beauty can be preserved by staying on approved trails, not littering, and adhering to the "Leave No Trace" principle.

10. Emergency Readiness:
Become acquainted with emergency protocols and the whereabouts of the closest medical facilities. Carry a basic first aid kit and let someone you can trust know about your itinerary, as cellular connectivity can be spotty.

11. Guided Tours and Activities:
One way to improve your comprehension of the historical and geological significance of the area is to take part in guided tours and activities. Speaking with informed guides deepens your connection to the environment and enhances your experience.

You can create the perfect environment for an incredible experience by carefully planning for your trip to Uluru-Kata Tjuta, where you can fully immerse yourself in the ethereal landscapes and historic wonders that await you in the center of Australia.

Traveling on a Budget

It's not necessary to spend a fortune traveling to Uluru-Kata Tjuta, Australia's breathtaking terrain. Here is a detailed guide to help you navigate this magnificent location on a budget.

1. Accommodation Choices: Select affordable lodging options close to Yulara, the entry point to Uluru-Kata Tjuta. For a more immersed experience, think about inexpensive hostels or camping areas.

2. Time is of Essence: If you visit between April and September, during the shoulder seasons, you'll enjoy warm weather and less tourists. This not only improves your experience but can also result in cost savings on your tour and lodging.

3. Self-Drive Experiences: Hiring a car can be an affordable option to see the Red Centre. You can choose your own speed and go off the usual route, finding hidden treasures along the way, thanks to its versatility.

4. Prepare Your Own Meals: Although there might not be many eating options, cooking your own food might help you save money. When staying in campgrounds or hostels, make use of the public kitchens, and remember to restock on supplies in larger towns prior to visiting Uluru-Kata Tjuta.

5. Free Activities and Hikes: In addition to nature's abundance of free offerings, there are several other activities available, such as stargazing and hiking. Make the most of the national park's many walking paths and self-guided activities.

6. Discount Cards and Passes: Explore the advantages of national park passes and discount cards in section six. These allow you to gain discounted admission to several attractions, so you can maximize your spending.

7. Cultural Experiences Without the Price Tag: Get fully immersed in the customs and traditions of the area without going over budget. Take advantage of the free cultural presentations and workshops offered by the national park to learn more about the area's rich Indigenous past.

8. Make Advance Reservation: To benefit from early-bird rates, reserve your trips and activities in advance. This helps you stay inside your budget and guarantees that you won't pass on well-liked activities.

Why Visit Uluru-Kata Tjuta?

Travelers from all over the world are drawn to Uluru-Kata Tjuta by its captivating scenery. These strong arguments will convince you that this famous location should be at the top of your list as you plan your travels for 2024.

1. Celestial Events:
Uluru-Kata Tjuta is an astronomical sanctuary, offering a plethora of celestial spectacles. This holy location offers an unearthly experience for stargazers and

astrophotographers alike with its low light pollution, making it the ideal vantage point for seeing lunar eclipses, meteor showers, and the starry night sky of the Southern Hemisphere.

2. Cultural Immersion:
Get fully engrossed in the rich indigenous culture of the Anangu people, who have historically tended this holy land. Offering a profound awareness of the area's spiritual significance, Uluru offers a unique opportunity to participate in special activities and cultural festivals that display old customs, dreamtime storytelling, and bright Aboriginal art.

3. Conservation Efforts:
Showcase the benefits of sustainable tourism practices in 2024 by endorsing continuing conservation projects. Your visit

helps the area's efforts to preserve its distinctive environment, which are actively being made. Participate in the campaign to save Uluru-Kata Tjuta's natural treasures for future generations.

4. Mild Weather and Perfect Conditions: Choosing a visit that coincides with ideal weather is essential. Enjoy the beautiful scenery without the excessive heat that makes outdoor exploration and activities more fun. Because of the moderate weather, your excursion will be comfortable and you'll be able to completely enjoy how beautiful the surrounds are.

5. Innovative interpretative Experiences: Uluru is anticipated to serve as a focal point for festivals and special events centered around Uluru-Kata Tjuta. This year offers a unique chance to plan your stay around

memorable experiences, such as stargazing gatherings and cultural celebrations. Don't miss the opportunity to participate in events that might not come around again, like a photography workshop, a special cultural performance, or a guided morning hike. To add even more brightness and excitement to your travel, go through the local calendar for activities that align with your interests.

6. Witness the Ever-Changing Colors: Uluru is transformed into a magnificent sight when the sun sets and rises over the Australian outback. From scorching reds to delicate purples, the old sandstone monolith's reflection of light produces a kaleidoscope of colors. When you travel, you may see this breathtaking natural show at its best, catching Uluru's magnificence in a variety of tones and moods, making every

moment a memorable and breathtaking experience

Chapter 2

Top Tourist Attractions in Uluru-Kata Tjuta

Uluru (Ayers Rock):
Take in the sight of the famous Uluru, a massive sandstone monolith that represents Australia's rich cultural past. Explore this holy site's spiritual importance for the Anangu people as the light creates vivid hues over its surface. Savor the breathtakingly beautiful color changes that occur at sunrise and sunset, highlighting the close relationship between the land and its native elders.

Kata Tjuta (The Olgas):

The mystical Kata Tjuta, sometimes called The Olgas, is a must-see sight. It is composed of 36 domes that rise sharply out of the red ground. Experience the immense magnitude of these age-old structures by starting the Valley of the Winds hike. Kata Tjuta's surreal geological marvels are not the only thing that draw visitors in; the wind-chase canyons also resound with spiritual stories.

Walpa Gorge:
The Walpa Gorge is a naturally occurring amphitheater surrounded by high rock walls. Come explore this wonderful place. Traverse the ravine, encircled by precipitous rocks, and feel the peace that envelops this undiscovered treasure. Be amazed by how the distinct vegetation is adjusting to this dry climate and experience the gorge's age-old vigor.

Mutitjulu Waterhole:

Start your trek to Mutitjulu Waterhole, an oasis at Uluru's base that has supported life for ages. Join the indigenous guides as they explore the cultural importance of this holy water spring by engaging with the stories carved into the rock walls. An insight of the profound bond between the Anangu people and their environment may be gained from the tranquility of the waterhole.

Aboriginal Cultural Center:

Visit the Aboriginal Cultural Center to fully immerse yourself in the Anangu people's live culture. Experience the world's oldest living culture via the vibrant display of traditional art, dance, and storytelling. Learn about Dreamtime stories from ancient times, interact with local artists, and get a deeper comprehension of the timeless customs that form Uluru-Kata Tjuta's spiritual web

Sunset and Sunrise Viewing Points:
As the sun sets and rises, take in the magnificent colors of Uluru and Kata Tjuta. Immersing tourists in the ethereal beauty of the Red Centre, the vivid hues flashing across the ancient rocks create a fascinating display.

Valley of the Winds:
Wander through the Valley of the Winds, where the untamed domes of Kata Tjuta are the backdrop for the symphony of nature. A sensory feast of wind-sculpted landscapes telling stories of the region's geological past may be found along the meandering trails that lead to panoramic views.

Mount Conner:

Mount Conner is a hidden jewel that provides a unique viewpoint of the Outback. Go off the usual road to visit it. For those seeking seclusion, this lesser-known monument offers a tranquil haven with its vast vistas and distinctive characteristics. It towers impressively.

Kings Canyon:

Experience the magnificence of Kings Canyon, a natural wonder characterized by soaring cliffs and verdant oases. In the middle of the dry environment, the Garden of Eden displays the tenacity of nature, and the picturesque rim walk offers breathtaking views.

The Majestic Monolith:

With its deep cultural importance, Uluru, the famous monolith, is considered the center of Australia. See its hallowed foundation, where rock art brings old Aboriginal tales to life. Observe the constantly shifting hues that mirror the spiritual nature of this magnificent monolith as the sun emits its warm charm.

Maruku Arts and Crafts: Experience the vibrant Indigenous culture there. Observe the production of traditional artworks that tell Dreamtime stories by interacting with local artisans. A special chance to learn about the Anangu people's background and bring home a little of their creative heritage is presented by this cultural center.

At each site in the center of Uluru-Kata Tjuta, a piece of Australia's ancient history is revealed, beckoning visitors to join the everlasting story etched in the vivid colors of the Red Centre.

Chapter 3

Best Transportation Guide

Getting to Uluru-Kata Tjuta

Experience breathtaking scenery and a diverse range of cultures on the journey to Uluru-Kata Tjuta, which is tucked away in the center of Australia. That famous place is isolated, but that doesn't stop people from coming; in fact, it makes the journey even more exciting. A thorough analysis of the top routes to Uluru-Kata Tjuta in 2024 can be seen below.

1. Air Travel:
The best effective strategy to begin your Uluru-Kata Tjuta experience is usually to take a plane to Ayers Rock Airport (Yulara

Airport). Nationwide accessibility is ensured by a number of domestic airlines that run frequent flights from key cities in Australia. Upon descending, the parched terrain below becomes an enchanting mosaic of old rock formations and red dirt.

2. Driving:
To explore the Australian Outback in greater detail, take a driving journey to Uluru-Kata Tjuta and discover its grandeur. Driving the famed Stuart Highway or seeing the picturesque Lasseter Highway are possible routes for the trip. Embrace the opportunity to see the shifting colors of the countryside during the trip, and be ready for extended periods of driving.

3. Guided Tours:
Selecting guided tours provides a level of practicality and knowledge of the area.

Transportation to Uluru-Kata Tjuta from major hubs is included in many tour companies' packages. This option offers opportunity to learn from professional guides about the history and cultural significance of the area in addition to guaranteeing a hassle-free travel.

4. The Ghan Expedition:
The Ghan Expedition is a magnificent rail trip that crosses Australia and offers a genuinely iconic experience. Travelers may continue their tour beyond Uluru-Kata Tjuta with this magnificent rail journey, which includes a stop at Alice Springs. The luxurious train offers an alternative travel experience, contrasting with the untamed beauty of the outback.

5. Charter Flights:

Charter flights provide a quick and beautiful substitute for individuals looking for exclusivity and a little more luxury. Travelers may save time on their journey and make the most of their time in Uluru-Kata Tjuta with direct flights to Ayers Rock Airport. People that are on a strict schedule or who like customized vacation experiences may find this choice very intriguing.

Getting Around Uluru-kata Tjuta

1. Shuttle Services:
Take advantage of the Uluru-Kata Tjuta shuttle service's convenience. Moving between important sites, such as Uluru and Kata Tjuta, is made hassle-free with the help of these services. They allow

passengers to explore at their own leisure because of their scheduled timetables.

2. Cycling Experiences: Choose a bike experience to really appreciate the area's untamed beauty. Riding the approved bike tracks surrounding Uluru and Kata Tjuta, you may rent a bicycle from one of the local companies. You may have a close relationship with the environment and have the flexibility to stop and take in the captivating surroundings when you choose this environmentally friendly alternative.

3. Guided Tours:
Take advantage of the knowledge that native tour guides have to offer by signing up for one. Insightful commentary on Uluru-Kata Tjuta's cultural importance and geological wonders is provided, and these trips frequently include transportation.

There are hidden jewels to be discovered, so whether you travel by bus or 4WD, guided trips provide a well selected experience.

4. Walking Trails:
Take a stroll along the well designated walking routes to really appreciate Uluru-Kata Tjuta's serene splendor. With alternatives for every level of fitness, these routes range in difficulty. Discover secret spots and take in Uluru's constantly shifting hues as you meander around the enchanted environment.

5. Self-Drive Exploration:
Renting a car gives adventurers the freedom to see Uluru-Kata Tjuta on their own terms. The area's well-maintained roads let you customize your route by stopping at vistas and sites that pique your interest.

6. Camel Tours:

Take a camel trip for a distinctive viewpoint of Australia's red center. Experience the majesty of the environment from a fresh viewpoint with these guided tours, which provide a unique form of transportation. Visiting important locations with informed guides who share cultural insights is a common feature of camel trips.

Take the approach that most appeals to your spirit of adventure, then set out on an extraordinary voyage.

Chapter 4

Best Accommodation Guide

The selection of lodging is an essential component of a pleasant and engaging trip to Uluru. In Australia's spiritual center, you'll discover the ideal location for lounging, whether you're looking for a little bit of luxury or the expansiveness of a campsite. Accommodation choices in Uluru-Kata Tjuta are varied and may accommodate different budgets and tastes.

1. Luxurious Resorts:
Sails in the Desert and Longitude 131 are two of the opulent resorts that encircle Uluru. Treat yourself to grandeur. The contemporary facilities and the outback's natural beauty are beautifully merged in

these enterprises. Enjoy excellent dining, indulging in spa treatments, and basking in the unmatched views of Uluru from the comfort of your tastefully decorated suite.

2. Camping Under the Stars: Excellent options for those looking for a more outdoorsy and daring experience are *Ayers Rock Resort Campground and Kings Creek Station*. Just picture yourself dozing off beneath the huge, starry Australian outback sky. Numerous campgrounds provide a range of amenities, from simple to luxurious, enabling guests to relax while still connecting with the natural world.

3. Cozy Desert Hotels: These hotels provide a distinctive lodging experience and frequently have architecture that blends nicely with the natural environment. Comfort and cultural

immersion come together harmoniously at these motels that embody the spirit of the outback with their little rooms.

4. Cultural Immersion in Indigenous Accommodations:

Like *Emu Walk Apartments and Desert Gardens Hotel*, you may fully immerse yourself in the rich indigenous traditions. Often including storytelling sessions, traditional art, and guided tours by educated indigenous hosts, these distinctive accommodations provide a genuine experience.

5. Self-Contained Apartments and Villas:

Families and parties may choose to stay in self-contained apartments or villas, such as those at *Emu Walk Apartments and The Lost Camel Hotel*. These lodgings provide the feeling of a home away from home because they have kitchens and living areas. Those who appreciate a more independent vacation experience and would rather have flexible meal alternatives should choose this option

6. Budget-Friendly Lodgings:
Ayers Rock Campground, Outback Hotel and Lodge, and Curtin Springs Wayside Inn are just a few of the affordable lodgings the Uluru-Kata Tjuta area has to offer visitors. These lodging options provide an economical option without sacrificing necessities, making them an ideal starting point for seeing the attractions of the Red Centre.

7. Eco-Friendly Lodgings:
By selecting eco-friendly lodging, you can help preserve the pristine ecosystem. These

environmentally friendly options put a high priority on reducing their environmental impact while still offering a comfortable and luxurious stay.

8. Family-Friendly Options: Taking a trip with close relatives? Choose kid-friendly lodgings like *Emu Walk Apartments* that provide amenities for every age. Ensuring a pleasant and pleasurable stay for families seeing Uluru-Kata Tjuta's attractions, these establishments provide large suites and recreational activities.

Where To Stay in Uluru-kata Tjuta

You should slow down and enjoy the moment right now. Experiencing Uluru and the Red Centre should not be hurried.

Reserve a place to stay and give yourself about a week to spend connecting with the locals and seeing their culture and way of life.

The whole Ayers Rock Resort, which is owned by Aboriginal people, has accommodations close to Uluru. A selection of lodging choices may be found here. Apartments on their own, an outback hotel, five-star luxury lodging, hotels, accommodations for backpackers, and a campground including campsites and cabins are all available. Shops, facilities, and regular guided tours to Uluru-Kata Tjuta National Park are available at the Ayers Rock Resort, which makes a good base.

The breathtaking sandstone walls of Kings Canyon are a must-see sight for any driver visiting the Red Centre. A working cattle and camel station offers you the option to camp, reserve a cheap bed, treat yourself to a luxurious accommodation, or spend the night in a remote wilderness lodge.

When you return from a day of exploration, lodging options will be there to greet you warmly.

1. Ayers Rock Campground ($43 - $185):

Nestled deep within the outback, Ayers Rock Campground provides reasonably priced camping options for those looking for an intimate experience with the natural world. It meets a range of preferences with both powered and unpowered sites and cabin accommodations. Budget-conscious travelers will find it to be an excellent option because of the amenities, which include shared bathrooms and a communal kitchen.

2. Sails in the Desert ($475 - $1100): Sails in the Desert offers the ultimate in luxury. In the outback, this luxurious resort offers a comfortable haven that blends modern conveniences with indigenous art. Everything about the hotel—from the large rooms to the fine dining—is designed to make your stay better. Beautiful views and easy access to the famous landmark are guaranteed by the resort's close proximity to Uluru.

3. Emu Walk Apartments ($420 - $680):

Comfort and convenience come together harmoniously at Emu Walk Apartments. These apartments, which have large living areas and fully equipped kitchens, are perfect for families or individuals who prefer independent living. The Emu Walk Apartments offer a warm haven following a day of exploration, with quick access to the town square and the Cultural Center.

4. Desert Gardens Hotel - Ayers Rock Resort ($400 - $530):

Desert Gardens Hotel provides views of Uluru and a peaceful haven amidst native gardens. An atmosphere of calm is created by the hotel's design, which blends in seamlessly with the surroundings. For a better experience, pick between cozy rooms and luxurious rock view rooms. Convenience is increased overall by being close to the resort's facilities.

5. The Lost Camel Hotel:

Enter The Lost Camel Hotel and lose yourself in modern outback elegance. This hotel provides an interesting and novel lodging choice with an emphasis on contemporary design and colorful decor. In the Ayers Rock Resort, The Lost Camel is a unique option. Take advantage of the pool, terrace, and eclectic atmosphere.

6. Longitude 131° ($1700 - $3400): Longitude 131° is a private retreat offering the height of luxury. With individualized service ensuring a smooth and luxurious stay, every elevated tent offers unhindered views of Uluru. Redefining outback luxury, this resort offers a special and personal connection to the surrounding natural wonders.

7. Discovery Resorts - Kings Canyon ($37 - $565):
Discovery Resorts - Kings Canyon offers various lodging choices for travelers

extending their adventure. This resort offers accommodations for a range of budgets, from luxurious cabins to inexpensive campsites. At night, unwind beneath the stars while taking in the untamed splendor of Kings Canyon during the day.

8. Outback Hotel and Lodge ($38 - $300):

the Outback Hotel and Lodge is a cozy haven for travelers looking for a more authentic outback experience. It boasts a rustic charm. For travelers on a tight budget who still want a taste of the real outback atmosphere, it's a great option because of its reasonable rates.

9. Kings Creek Station ($26 - $920): The operational cattle and camel ranch Kings Creek ranch has a variety of lodging

choices, ranging from rustic camping to opulent safari accommodations. Enjoy the breathtaking surroundings of this exceptional station while losing yourself in the outback way of life.

10. Curtin Springs Wayside Inn ($5 - $360):

With prices ranging from $5 to $360, this place offers a genuine bush experience. Affordable lodging options are available at this family-run business, which offers both rooms and campsites. While visiting Uluru-Kata Tjuta, you should not miss the true outback environment and wonderful friendliness.

11. Discovery Parks - Kings Canyon ($50 - $180):

Nestled in close proximity to Kings Canyon, Discovery Parks - Kings Canyon provides a range of lodging choices. It meets a range of interests, including powered caravan sites as well as cozy cottages. While visiting the Kings Canyon, take use of the shared amenities and experience the area's natural beauties.

Things To Do In Uluru

1. Take a walk around Uluru
A wheelchair-accessible majority of the six designated paths around Uluru allow you to retrace the pathways of your Aboriginal ancestors. Rangers narrate the history of the Mala (rufous hare-wallaby) people on the free Mala Walk, which stretches the length of Uluru's base—two kilometers each way. The 10.6km base trek around the rock offers views of Uluru's whole natural and cultural splendour.

2. Take in the artwork at Field of Light. Experience the Field of Light art installation's colorful display of the desert lighting up in the pre-dawn light or as darkness descends onto Uluru at dusk. The world-renowned phenomena created by British artist Bruce Munro illuminates an area equivalent to seven football fields with around 50,000 solar-powered spheres. "Looking at lots of beautiful lights" is how the local Pitjantjatjara people refer to it, Tili Wiru Tjuta Nyakutjaku.

3. Step around the Some of Kata Tjuta
See Kata Tjuta, a group of 36 steep domes located 20 minutes' drive west of Uluru, by putting on your walking boots. Walk 600m to the dune observation point for a panoramic view, then follow the 2.6km return Walpa Gorge trail to experience it all. Go on a 7.4-kilometer trek around the

Valley of the Winds to experience the core of Kata Tjuta, which is really 200 meters higher than Uluru. Alternatively, stroll among unique vegetation to a spearwood forest.

4. Enjoy the Sounds of Silence
Uluru's three-course Sounds of Silence supper offers the ultimate starry dining experience. While Uluru's colors shift with the sunset light, enjoy canapés and sparkling champagne atop a red desert dune. Then enjoy superb Australian wine coupled with delights inspired by bush tucker. The Australian night sky's planets and galaxies come to life after supper, courtesy of an astronomer.

5. Take a walk around Kings Canyon
After a three-hour journey from Uluru, start early to tackle the 3.5-hour rim hike of

150-meter-tall sandstone cliff, Kings Canyon, in Watarrka National Park. A green "Garden of Eden" lies in the canyon bottom, accessible only after a strenuous 500-step climb that rewards you with views over verdant woods and waterholes from the peak. Alternatively follow the gentler, shaded creek path through the bottom of the canyon.

6. Dine "Under a Desert Moon" Treat yourself to a 5-course meal served outside beneath the stars, with the only lighting coming from the flickering fire and the moon (available April through October) at Kings Canyon Resort. Fresh Australian cuisine, such as wild barramundi from the Northern Territory and free-range emu koftas, forms the foundation of the menu. There is an eight pair maximum, which ensures intimacy.

7. Make contact with local Maruku artists
A collection of over 900 Anangu artists from 20 isolated desert settlements around Uluru, Maruku Arts offers workshops in dot painting and wood carving with indigenous artists. Discuss local bush medicine, the meanings included into the artwork, and desert customs with the artists while you sit down with them. A few Pitjantjatjara terms may perhaps become apparent to you.

8. Use a Segway, fly, or ride a bike
Explore Uluru-Kata Tjuta National Park in ways other than on foot. Take a tandem jump for the more daring, or explore the city's landmarks from above while riding a camel tour at sunrise or sunset. For the perfect sunset tour or a short 30-minute ride, hop on the back of a Harley Davidson motorbike or a three-wheeled trike. You

may rent a bike and tour Uluru at your own speed or cruise around the monument on a Segway.

9. Pick an item from the Wintjiri Arts and Museum
Visit Wintjiri Arts and Museum, an Aboriginal art exhibition at Ayers Rock Resort with artwork from Pitjantjatjara and Ngaanyatjarra lands artists in residence. Choose something unique to bring home from art to soaps, cosmetics, and bush medicine, and peruse the local history exhibits while watching artists at work.

10. Attend a paper-making tour in Curtin Springs
A thriving outback cattle ranch located one hour's drive from Uluru, Curtin Springs is where you may hand make your own paper from natural grasses. Discover the many

grasses, including spinifex, oat grass, woollybutt, kangaroo, and kerosene, and how they're made into paper by taking part in a one-hour tour or a two-day workshop. The lengthier session will involve cutting, pulping, and pressing the grass to make a unique memento to bring home.

Chapter 5

Culinary Delights, Regional Specialties, and Restaurants

Savor the colorful gastronomic mosaic of Uluru-Kata Tjuta, where every morsel narrates a tale of the historic region. Start your food adventure with the famous Bush Tucker, which features local delicacies such as quandong, bush tomatoes, and kangaroo. Welcome to Tali Wiru, where contemporary Australian food combines with Indigenous flavours to provide a distinctive dining experience beneath the stars. Try these must-try meals to experience the essence of Indigenous history as you set off on a gastronomic adventure.

Local Cuisines

1. Tasting Plate of Bush Tucker at Walpa Bar

A Bush Tucker Tasting Plate, a blend of local delicacies, is a great way to start your culinary journey. Savor flavors that offer a distinct perspective on traditional Aboriginal cuisine, such as quandong, bush tomatoes, and native herbs.

2. Kangaroo and Emu Specialties at Tali Wiru

Savor dishes made from kangaroo and emu to truly feel the spirit of the Outback. Perfectly cooked to medium-rare, these tender cuts of meat provide a unique flavour that captivates the senses and the imagination.

3. The Willy Wonka-esque chocolate fountain at Ilkari Restaurant

Get ready to push your way to the front of the line for this particular culinary experience. Part of the extensive buffet offered by the hotel restaurant is this enormous, multi-tiered fountain of luscious and beautiful chocolaty bliss. Though, let's be honest, you'll give in to your inner child and go right for the candy and more chocolate. There is the symbolic matching of fruit on skewers to dip into it.

4. Didgeridoo Dining:

At Didgeridoo Dining, traditional Aboriginal ingredients are expertly paired with modern cooking methods to delight your palate. Let your senses dance with the special blend of indigenous spices, such lemon myrtle and wattleseed, which turns every dish into a perfect symphony of tastes.

5. Barramundi with Macadamia Pesto: Enjoy the aromas of the nearby waterways with Barramundi, a delicious freshwater fish, served with Macadamia Pesto. This dish, enhanced with a macadamia pesto, is an example of how Indigenous foods may be combined with contemporary cooking techniques.

6. Wattleseed Ice Cream:
Serve Wattleseed Ice Cream to finish your dinner sweetly. With its nutty taste of wattleseed, this delicacy honors the local flora and adds a wonderful touch to your culinary excursion.

7. Croc dog at Pioneer BBQ and Bar

Excellent and very "grammable"! This unusual hot dog made with crocodile meat tastes really delicious, is probably healthier than the actual thing, and will make you proud to eat it for weeks.

8. Quandong Pie:

Try a Quandong Pie to explore the world of desserts. This classic Australian pastry has a lasting, mouthwatering taste that is well balanced by the tartness of quandong, a native bush fruit.

9. The Outback's Bounty: Fresh Produce and Seafood

Bask in the wealth of the Outback, where delectable seafood and fresh produce reign supreme. A genuinely unique culinary experience is provided by the flavorful yabbies and locally sourced barramundi, where each bite captures the essence of the surrounding landscapes

10. Bush Damper at Desert Awakenings
Australian bread known as "Bush Damper," baked over a campfire, is a mainstay in outback villages. It is a must-try because of its flavorful and hearty rustic charm. Whether eaten on its own or with locally produced jams and spreads, this straightforward yet tasty bread honors the ingenuity and tenacity of the area's first residents.

11. Saltbush Lamb:
This culinary marvel will tantalize your palate and highlight the area's dedication to ethical and sustainable farming methods. The meat offers a delightful glimpse into the region's farming practices, with its subtle notes of saltbush interwoven

throughout for a juicy and tender dining experience.

12. MacDonnell Ranges Bush Honey: Indulge in a taste of the sweet on your travels. This honey, which was harvested from the natural vegetation around the well-known MacDonnell Ranges, has a distinct and deep flavor. This golden nectar captures the spirit of the desert, whether it is served with regional cheeses or poured over desserts.

Restaurants, Bars And Cafes

1. Tali Wiru

Location: Center of Ayers Rock National Park

Description: Under the expansive Outback sky, Tali Wiru is the epitome of excellent dining, providing a singular experience.

This upscale alfresco eatery features locally sourced ingredients in each dish on its painstakingly created menu, which is inspired by Indigenous cuisines. Guests experience a symphony of tastes, flawless service, and an ambiance that is nothing short of breathtaking as the sun sets over Uluru.

2. Bough House Restaurant
Location: Outback Pioneer Hotel and Lodge
Description: Bough House Restaurant is a sanctuary for people looking for a tasteful fusion of fine food with the natural beauty of the Outback. With expansive windows framing views of Uluru, the restaurant's architecture blends seamlessly with the natural surroundings. The menu features a blend of cuisine with both international and local influences, providing a varied gastronomic experience in the peaceful

setting. Breakfast is served daily, and dinner is served periodically.

3. Mangata Bistro & Bar
Location: Desert Gardens Hotel
Description: Mangata Bistro Bar offers a large menu featuring both Australian and foreign flavors, all in a laid-back bistro setting. It's a favorite among those looking for a relaxed yet elegant dining experience because the outdoor seating area allows customers to enjoy their meals in the natural surroundings. Open for dinner, lunch, and breakfast. Make reservations in advance.

4. Sounds of Silence Restaurant:
Location: Yulara
Description: Sounds of Silence offers a dining experience that is unmatched, despite not being a typical restaurant. This

outdoor feast offers a gourmet treat buffet matched with the best Australian wines, all set against the stunning backdrop of Uluru. The stars come alive as the evening wears on, forming a cosmic canopy over the diners—a memorable fusion of stargazing and dining.

5. Ilkari Restaurant

Location: Sails in the Desert

Description: Inspired by Uluru-Kata Tjuta's timeless landscapes, Ilkari Restaurant exudes elegance and grace. Ilkari is distinguished by its use of fresh, seasonal foods and a menu that reflects the variety of flavors found in the area. The chic design, embellished with Native American artwork, offers a sophisticated environment for visitors to savor gastronomic and visual treats. Breakfast and dinner are served there. Make reservations in advance.

6. Pira Pool Bar

Location: Sails in the Desert

Description: The welcoming sanctuary by the pool at Pira Pool Bar invites you to unwind and enjoy a refreshing experience. This relaxed location is ideal for indulging in light fare and cool drinks, fostering a relaxed ambiance that goes well with long afternoons spent soaking up the desert sun. Accessible from mid-morning until dusk.

7. Walpa Lobby Bar

Location: Sails in the Desert

Description: Walpa Lobby Bar provides a sumptuous environment for visitors to relax and enjoy fine beverages. Enjoying expertly made cocktails, fine wines, and a variety of fine spirits is made even more enjoyable by the panoramic windows of the bar, which offer breathtaking views of the surrounding landscapes. Open from first light until last light.

8. Kulata Academy Café
Location: Uluru-Kata Tjuta Cultural Centre
Description: Kulata Academy Café is a secret treasure for anyone looking for a real Indigenous food experience. Owned and run by the Anangu community, this cafe offers both contemporary and traditional bush tucker. Take in the vivid tales and artwork that adorn the Cultural Center as they indulge in dishes like wattleseed damper and delicacies infused with lemon myrtle. Lunch and breakfast are served here. There is takeout available.

9. Arnguli Grill & Restaurant
Location: Desert Gardens Hotel
Description: The Arnguli Grill is a modern eatery that skillfully combines Indigenous

ingredients with modern cooking methods. With items like saltbush and kangaroo fillet, the cuisine highlights the distinctive tastes of the area. The restaurant's warm and inviting setting, along with breathtaking views of Uluru, produces a dining experience that is both culturally rich and visually captivating. Open for dinner only. Make reservations in advance.

10. Geckos Café

Location: Town square in Yulara
Description: Geckos Café offers a laid-back ambiance with a panoramic background of Kata Tjuta. The cuisine boasts a broad selection, from full breakfasts to tasty lunches. Whether having a leisurely meal or getting a quick bite, this café encapsulates the essence of Outback eating, making it a popular among both locals and foreigners.

Open for lunch and dinner. There is takeout available.

11. Ayers Wok Noodle Bar
Location: Ayers Rock Resort
Description: Ayers Wok Noodle Bar
At Uluru-Kata Tjuta, the Ayers Wok Noodle Bar adds a hint of Asian flavour to the local cuisine. Wok-tossed noodles, stir fries, and other Asian-inspired dishes are served at this lively restaurant. For those seeking a quick and flavorful meal, it's a popular option because of its casual setting. Daily dinner service and lunches are available seasonally. Only the takeaway

12. Ininti Cafe and Souvenirs
Location: Uluru-Kata Tjuta Cultural Centre
Description: In addition to satisfying gastronomic desires, Ininti Cafe offers a chance to learn about Indigenous art and

culture. This cafe is perfect for refueling while immersing oneself in the rich heritage of the Anangu people. It is located within the Cultural Centre and serves a variety of light meals, snacks, and beverages.

13. Pioneer BBQ and Bar
Location: Outback Pioneer Hotel and Lodge
Description: Pioneer BBQ and Bar's substantial barbecue selections perfectly encapsulate the essence of Outback dining. The aroma of grilled specialties fills the air as people congregate around communal tables, creating a convivial atmosphere. This is the place to go if you're in the mood for traditional barbecue flavors in a welcoming atmosphere. Until late, starting at 11:00 a.m.

14. Outback Pioneer Kitchen
Location: Outback Pioneer Hotel and Lodge

Description: Are you not feeling like doing anything fancy? Great salads, sandwiches, wraps, pizzas, and burgers can be found at this affordable restaurant. daily lunch and dinner hours.

Pubs in Uluru

Explore Uluru's diverse selection of bars and pubs to fully immerse yourself in the city's vibrant social scene. These places give visitors a distinctive look at the local way of life in addition to refreshing concoctions.

1. The Outback Tap House
The Outback Tap House is a laid-back yet energetic drinking spot, nestled against the breathtaking silhouette of Uluru. This pub is a favorite among both locals and visitors because of its large selection of craft beers and ciders. With a cold drink in hand, take

a seat outside on the terrace, take in the stunning views, and relish the moment.

2. Red Sands Lounge
Visit the Red Sands Lounge for a more sophisticated experience. With its carefully chosen menu of signature cocktails made with locally sourced ingredients, this upscale restaurant puts a contemporary spin on classic flavors. It's the perfect place for an intimate night out or a laid-back evening with friends because of the cozy seating and ambient lighting.

3. Kata Tjuta Pub
The Kata Tjuta Pub, which is located outside of Uluru, has a rustic charm that perfectly embodies the Australian outback. Enter to find a welcoming environment where neighbors congregate to tell tales over a pint. On some nights, live music is

also presented at the pub, offering a genuine taste of the local entertainment scene.

4. Desert Spirits Bar

Check out the Desert Spirits Bar for a distinctive fusion of culture and mixed cocktails. This place takes pride in presenting regional flavors and spirits. Drink carefully made cocktails that are based on age-old formulas, and allow the knowledgeable bartenders to take you on a sensory excursion. The atmosphere is enhanced with a layer of authenticity by the indigenous art that adorns it.

5. Sunset Saloon

Get a captivating view of the sun setting behind Uluru by heading to the Sunset Saloon as the day draws to an end. This alfresco bar offers a refreshing drink selection and a prime location to witness nature's spectacle. It's the ideal place to relax after exploring for the day while taking in the breathtaking scenery with other tourists.

6. Rock & Roll Bar:
This exciting venue is perfect for individuals looking for a livelier, more vibrant atmosphere. This pub is a center of activity, with live music resonating against the old rocks. Guests may enjoy handcrafted cocktails influenced by the region's rich cultural tapestry while dancing the night away beneath the starry desert sky.

Chapter 6

Uluru-Kata Tjuta's Cultural and Natural History

The Anangu People and Culture

The heart of Uluru-Kata Tjuta's mystique is the Anangu People and their unique culture. The Anangu are the traditional occupants of this sacred territory, having tended it for tens of thousands of years. Every part of their lives is intertwined with their relationship to the vivid red dirt and massive rock formations.

1. Ancient Wisdom:

With a deep spiritual connection, the Anangu have a sophisticated knowledge of their environment. Their elaborate oral traditions, passed down from generation to generation, describe the formation of Uluru and Kata Tjuta, assigning to primordial creatures every curve and crack. This tradition of storytelling acts as a manual for sustainable living in balance with the environment in addition to teaching cultural information.

2. Tjukurpa – Law and Lore:
The spiritual, social, and natural principles that govern life are encompassed in the Tjukurpa, which is fundamental to Anangu culture. It inspires a comprehensive way of living in harmony with nature, influencing their rituals, artwork, and daily activities. The Anangu preserve the Tjukurpa for future generations by graphically articulating it through bright symbols and elaborate dot paintings.

3. Sacred Sites: Representing live reservoirs of Anangu spiritual energy, Uluru and Kata Tjuta are highly significant sacred sites. It is strongly recommended that visitors honor the cultural sensitivity of specific areas and follow the guided tours given by Anangu elders. In addition to being natural wonders, these sacred locations represent the Anangu people's deep spiritual ties.

4. The Anangu Dreamtime Stories: The dreamtime stories of the Anangu people are the sacred tales that support the cultural identity of the Anangu people spiritually. Told for countless years, these myths explain how the earth, the planet, and all living things came to be. These stories provide Uluru-Kata Tjuta its distinct meaning, connecting the natural world to the spiritual plane. Dreamtime stories

outline the moral and ethical standards that drive Anangu life and provide an explanation of the origins of the components in nature. They function as a thorough guide. By means of complex oral storytelling and expressive art forms, the Anangu people preserve these age-old stories, promoting a deep bond between the contemporary community and the eternal spiritual elements ingrained in the difficult terrain they inhabit.

5. Cultural Practices:
Dance, dot painting, carving, and other artistic mediums are some of the ways that Anangu culture is expressed. These manifestations act as a medium for narratives, emphasizing how crucial it is to preserve their history. Guests have the chance to interact with Anangu artists,

learning about their methods of creation and the backstories of their creations.

6. Rituals and Ceremonies

The Anangu hold rituals and ceremonies to honor life's cycles, the varying seasons, and significant life events. The Anangu people's connection to their surroundings is strengthened by these ceremonies, which are frequently accompanied by traditional dances and singing. Those who are lucky enough to be there at these events are able to see the tremendous spiritual depth of Anangu culture.

7. Difficulties and Resilience:

The effects of colonization and modernity have been among the difficulties the Anangu People have had to deal with. They yet continue to uphold their ties to the land and cultural identity. Their continued dedication to protecting their culture and promoting Indigenous rights is demonstrated by projects like the Uluru Statement from the Heart.

Understanding the significance of Uluru-Kata Tjuta requires a thorough examination of the rich tapestry of Anangu People and Culture. In the vivid red heart of Australia, it is an immersion into a living history, where the past, present, and future come together.

Geological History

The fascinating story of Uluru-Kata Tjuta's geological past weaves together eons of natural processes that have produced this renowned Australian landscape. Thick layers of sand and sediment accumulated approximately 600 million years ago during the Neoproterozoic era, eventually forming the forerunner to Uluru and Kata Tjuta.

A phase of uplift and folding occurred in the region some 500 million years ago, shaping the geological base that would eventually give rise to these enormous monoliths. Gradually, erosion, like a diligent artisan, carved away at the surrounding terrain to unveil the magnificent structures that we admire to this day.

The sandstone monolith Uluru serves as a reminder of the strength of the elements—wind and water. Millennia of weathering have left its unique vertical grooves cut into its surface, giving it a captivating texture that shifts color with the light. With each dome symbolizing a distinct chapter in the region's geological story, Kata Tjuta, a collection of domed rock formations, tells a parallel story of geological evolution.

The distinctive red color that envelops Uluru-Kata Tjuta is a consequence of iron minerals embedded in the sandstone. The already captivating scenery is enhanced by its distinctive tint, which is especially striking at sunrise and dusk.

The area underwent more geological changes throughout the millennia, and the Anangu people—the land's original custodians—became deeply connected to it. The cultural fabric of the Anangu people and Uluru-Kata Tjuta are inextricably linked, resulting in a setting where the natural and cultural narratives coexist peacefully and reveal a complex web of interconnectedness.

This geological symphony is enhanced by the nearby treasure, Watarrka National Park. The Red Centre boasts an additional layer of geological richness due to its rocky topography and the famed Kings Canyon, which serve as a display for the ongoing processes of erosion and sedimentation.

Flora and Fauna of Uluru-Kata Tjuta

Uluru-Kata Tjuta's colorful tapestry is woven by a wide variety of flora and fauna that flourish in this desert environment, in addition to old rocks and a rich cultural legacy.

Flora (Plant life):
A diverse range of hardy plants that are specially suited to the severe weather can

be seen growing in the red desert sands that envelop Uluru and Kata Tjuta. The prickly blades of spinifex grass, which covers much of the parched plains, are what give the scene its distinctive red color. In contrast to the ochre boulders, ghost gums are silent sentinels with their smooth white bark.

Among the amazing flora, the Mulga tree is particularly noteworthy. The Mulga offers a variety of animal cover and food with its gnarled branches and silvery leaves. During rainy seasons, delicate wildflowers like the vivid Desert Pea bloom quickly, bringing fleeting bursts of color to the rocky landscape.

Fauna (Wildlife):
A refuge for a wide variety of species, Uluru-Kata Tjuta is more than just a geological marvel. Spotting kangaroos and

wallabies grazing on the scant flora is possible because they are acclimated to the arid environment. With grace and subtlety, the Perentie lizard traverses the red dirt. It is a fearsome predator.

The resident birds, which include the famous Australian wedge-tailed eagle soars high overhead, will please birdwatchers. Fluttering amid the desert bushes is the Zebra Finch, while the elusive Spinifex Pigeon, with its delicate plumage, conceals in the shadows of the rocks.

The chirps of the inland frog species and the gentle rustle of the Brush-tailed Mulgara provide life to the nocturnal world. With its characteristic long snout, the endangered marsupial known as the Bilby forages for food beneath the expansive, starry desert sky.

While exploring Uluru-Kata Tjuta, pause to observe the complex interactions between the plants and wildlife, which serve as a monument to the adaptation and resilience of life in Australia's magnificent red center.

Watarrka National Park

Watarrka National Park, tucked away in the country's center, is a monument to Australia's varied and breathtaking landscapes. With its high cliffs, narrow canyons, and vivid vegetation, this natural wonder—home to the well-known Kings Canyon—captivates tourists. Millions of years are depicted in the park's old geological formations, which you can explore.

1. Geological Marvels:

Watarrka National Park is a geological wonder, exemplified by Kings Canyon's soaring sandstone walls. These magnificent cliffs, sculpted by the passage of time, rise sharply and create a maze of rough terrain that entices daring people to explore. Discover the elaborate domes and cracks that invite visitors to observe Earth's history carved in stone and tell stories of ancient geological processes.

2. Aboriginal Connection:
Discover the cultural core of Watarrka National Park, where the natural environment is woven with the legends of the Luritja and Pertame people. The deep spiritual significance of Watarrka to the Anangu people is revealed in this section, which also examines the Dreamtime stories and sacred sites that have been passed down through the generations. Discover the

close bond that exists between the land and its indigenous guardians, whose history is engraved in every crack and stone.

3. Magnificent Flora and Fauna

Watarrka National Park is home to rare plants and animals in addition to its geological wonders. Native plant species that have adapted to the dry climate highlight the tenacity of nature. Watch out for the rare black-footed rock wallaby, which inhabits the park. Birdwatchers will enjoy seeing wedge-tailed eagles soar overhead, lending the wide skies a hint of untamed elegance.

4. Cultural Importance

Beyond its inherent beauty, Watarrka is significant because the Luritja and Pertame people, the land's traditional custodians, view it as culturally significant. Dreamtime stories, which describe how the surrounding formations came to be and offer a spiritual background for the canyon's majesty, are ingrained with references to their connection to the land.

5. Kings Canyon Rim Walk:
Set out on the well-known Kings Canyon Rim Walk to discover the park's breath-taking vistas. With views of the magnificent Amphitheatre and the Garden of Eden, this section leads you along the winding trail. Seize the spirit of this journey, where each step is a dialogue with the historic terrain and the wide-open vistas inspire awe and humility.

Immerse yourself in the Anangu people's living cultural tapestry while you explore Watarrka National Park. Guided tours provide you with a deep understanding of the symbiotic relationship between the land and its custodians, as well as insights into the ancient stories and traditions that have been passed down through the generations.

Interestingly, Watarrka is a dynamic ecosystem that adjusts to the seasonal fluctuations rather than just being a static landscape. Rarely occurring periods of rain cause the park to change, with water tumbling down the canyon walls and briefly forming oases in this desolate area.

Reaching far beyond the well-beaten paths, Watarrka National Park invites visitors to establish a deep connection with the natural world. The park offers an incredible chapter in your exploration of the Red Centre, leaving an enduring impression on your journey through the heart of Australia, regardless of your attraction—its geological wonders, varied wildlife, or cultural significance.

Chapter 7

Outdoor Activities in Uluru-Kata Tjuta

1. Hiking in Uluru-Kata Tjuta: Exploring the several hiking routes in Uluru-Kata Tjuta will take you on an incredible hike across the area's ancient landscapes. As you wind across the ochre-colored landscape, these paths provide a close-up view of the holy locations. Uluru's cultural significance is revealed through Indigenous rock art and stories along the Kuniya Walk, which circles the base of the rock. A more strenuous experience awaits you when you trek Kata Tjuta's Valley of the Winds, where

you may take in the breathtaking splendor of the domed rock formations.

2. Camel Tours:

Take a camel ride for a truly unique perspective of the Red Centre. Take in the calm view of the expansive surroundings as you gently sway atop these magnificent animals as they travel across the desert. Uluru's shifting hues at sunrise or sunset can be peacefully viewed with the accompaniment of the camels' rhythmic footfall and the serenity of the desert. Enjoy the guides' captivating narration as they offer historical perspectives on the region and the role that camels played in Australian desert exploration.

3. Helicopter Tours:

Take a helicopter tour to get an amazing aerial view of Uluru and Kata Tjuta, which will enhance your experience of these famous sites. Take in Uluru's enormous size and Kata Tjuta's characteristic domes as you soar over the vast crimson plains. The geological marvels and cultural significance of these ancient formations will become clearly apparent to you as the helicopter flies overhead. Embark on experiences that will last a lifetime by capturing expansive vistas that seem to go on forever.

4. Stargazing:
With the sun setting, Uluru-Kata Tjuta's vast desert sky becomes a celestial painting. Explore the fascinating realm of stargazing in this chapter. The pristine Outback skies provide an amazing view of the stars, planets, and other celestial wonders when you're away from the lights of the city. Accompany escorted stargazing events to discover the constellations of the Southern

Hemisphere and discover historic Indigenous tales interwoven into the night sky.

5. Photography:
Through the lens of your camera, capture the spirit of Uluru and Kata Tjuta. Every moment is worthy of being captured on camera, from the vivid hues of sunrise and sunset illuminating the famous monoliths with a warm glow to the way light and shadows dance to highlight the untamed landscapes. In order to capture the breathtaking beauty of this red heartland in your photographs, find the best locations and pick up photographic tricks.

6. Birdwatching:
Experience birdwatching in the center of Australia by going on an avian exploration expedition. Birdwatchers will find a wealth

of different bird species in the area surrounding Uluru-Kata Tjuta. Experience the distinct landscape while observing colorful parrots, imposing eagles, and other indigenous avian species in their native range. The vivid birdlife against the backdrop of the desert terrain makes for an enthralling encounter, regardless of your level of skill as a birder.

7. Aboriginal Guided Tours:
It offers a deep connection to the age-old tales and customs of the Anangu people. Take part in a cultural journey with them. Experience the mystical significance of Uluru and Kata Tjuta with these informative tours led by expert Indigenous guides. Experience the rich cultural legacy ingrained in this magnificent site by taking a stroll around the holy grounds, listening

to Dreamtime narratives, and seeing traditional ceremonies.

Chapter 8

Uluru's Art and Cultural Scene

Art Galleries and Museums

Discover the thriving art scene in the center of the Red Centre of Australia. There are many interesting art galleries in Uluru-Kata Tjuta, each providing a different perspective on the region's rich cultural diversity. These galleries highlight the region's rich cultural diversity with everything from modern creations to masterpieces by the native people.

1. Maruku Arts Cultural Centre:

Visit Maruku Arts Cultural Centre to immerse yourself in the Anangu people's vibrant culture. This place exhibits the artistic talent that has been passed down through the years by effortlessly fusing traditional and contemporary art. Admire the exquisite dot paintings, each one narrating a story about the Dreamtime and the strong bond with the land.

2. Uluru-Kata Tjuta Cultural Centre: Visit the Uluru-Kata Tjuta Cultural Centre to immerse yourself in the essence of indigenous tradition. This hub, which houses an amazing collection of art that captures the continuing spirit of the community, acts as a protector of Anangu traditions. The center captures the spirit of a civilization that is profoundly ingrained in the terrain, from colorful canvases to expertly produced antiques.

3. Walkatjara Art Gallery:
Visit Walkatjara Art Gallery to see canvases that capture the rich orange tones of the surrounding countryside. Works by Anangu artists are on display in this gallery, demonstrating their close ties to the earth. The sculptures' rich intricacies and vivid hues take the viewer on a visual tour of Uluru and Kata Tjuta's spiritual significance.

4. Gallery of Central Australia (GoCA)
Another Uluru art destination is the Gallery of Central Australia (GoCA), which is situated at Ayers Rock Resort close to the Desert Gardens Hotel and features works by both established and up-and-coming artists. Along with other carefully chosen goods, Punu and other locally produced artwork are available here. This cultural

centre uses stimulating art talks and rotating exhibitions to inform and excite its guests about Uluru Aboriginal art.

Furthermore, an artist-in-residence program is currently in place, wherein artists spend the entire day working in the gallery. It is at this time that they are allowed to create, exhibit, and sell their artwork. The gallery's genuine artwork is available for purchase by visitors. You may help the family of artists working in the central desert region by buying this artwork.

5. Aboriginal Rock Art

The Aboriginal rock art of Uluru is another kind of art to behold. Old Tjukurpa stories are portrayed in this rock art. The rock art sites are covered in layers of various images, symbols, and figures. The fact that rock surfaces overlap indicates that Anangu people have been using these rocks for instruction for tens of thousands of years. These designs in the sand and rock art are used by the Anangu to teach their creation stories. The Uluru rock paintings provide historical and scientific proof that people have lived in this region. I think the artwork is at least 30,000 years old.

6. Wintjiri Arts and Museum:
Dr. Dawn Casey, Chairperson of Indigenous Land Corporation, unveiled the Wintjiri Arts & Museum at Ayers Rock Resort. Its sole purpose is to exhibit and promote regional Indigenous art. Art lovers are drawn to Wintjiri Arts & Museum by its distinctive fusion of historical relics and visual narratives. See the fusion of modern Aboriginal art with the historical narratives that have shaped this hallowed territory.

The museum's displays highlight the development of artistic expression while also illuminating the connections between spirituality, culture, and the arts.

Festivals and Events

The Uluru-Kata Tjuta region offers guests an immersive experience through its festivals, which weave a vibrant tapestry of cultural diversity. These gatherings create a unique fusion of celebration and tradition, showcasing the close ties that exist between the indigenous people and the land.

1. Tjungu Festival (April)

A family-friendly celebration spanning four days. named after the Pitjantjatjara word meaning "gathering together" or "meeting." An important event on the cultural calendar is the Tjungu Festival. Through art, dance, and music, it brings together Indigenous and non-Indigenous groups to promote understanding. Visitors get a rare look at the Anangu people's living culture through storytelling, traditional rites, and modern performances.

2. Parrtjima - Festival in Light (April)
Parrtjima, which translates to "lighting up" or "shining," is a captivating light festival that turns a desert night into a rainbow of hues. This yearly event is a visual feast that combines state-of-the-art light installations with ancient stories to illuminate the environment surrounding Uluru and connect with the spiritual essence of the area. It is an amazing examination of the meeting point of modernism and tradition.

3. Uluru Camel Cup (May)

The Camel Cup gives the desert scenery a dash of whimsical fun. This eccentric event draws both locals and visitors, though it is not just for indigenous people. This festival is known for its lively atmosphere, live music, and racing camels. It demonstrates how the area can embrace both its long-standing customs and modern pleasures.

4. Australian Outback Marathon (July)
Running through the red planes is a global event that takes place against the breathtaking backdrop of Uluru/Ayers Rock.

5. Uluru Astronomy Weekend (August)
The spectacular outback night sky is highlighted by the event. Stargazing opportunities and talks about astrophysics are among the activities of the event, which

is hosted by Dr. Karl Kruszelnicki and attended by other international experts in the field of astronomy.

6. Uluru Festival (March, August & November)

As a part of Ayers Rock Resort's BushTucker Journeys, this brand-new quarterly culinary event honors the native flavors of Australia. Along with open-air fine dining and traditional bush tucker tastings, the gastronomic weekend celebrates Indigenous food and culture. It also features a signature masterclass and a three-course tasting dinner under the stars with Indigenous celebrity chef Mark Olive, the ambassador for Bush Tucker Journeys.

7. Uluru Wellness Retreat (September)

With practical mindfulness workshops, silence survival techniques, intuition and intention tips, Qigong workshops, and guided meditations to improve one's life, this transformational weekend, hosted by well-known life change facilitator Peter Bliss, enables participants to master their minds and manage their emotions. This rejuvenating weekend is set in the spiritual surrounds of Uluru-Kata Tjuta National Park and Ayers Rock Resort. It includes a nourishing and healthy food program, as well as the option to dine al fresco in the desert.

8. Desert Dreaming Yoga Festival (April)

A unique fusion of yoga, mindfulness, and connection to the land is offered by the Desert Dreaming Yoga Festival for those looking for a more tranquil experience. Participants engage in holistic practices against the backdrop of Kata Tjuta, fully submerging themselves in the spiritual energy of Australia's outback.

These festivals offer more than just entertainment; they also serve as a means of comprehending Uluru-Kata Tjuta's immense cultural significance. Every festival in this magnificent red heart of Australia adds a new dimension to the tapestry of experiences, whether you're dancing beneath the stars or taking in the vastness of the desert.

Wildlife

The untamed beauty of Uluru-Kata Tjuta's wildlife, a monument to the adaptability and resiliency of life in the heart of Australia's red wilderness, will enchant you as you explore the area.

1. Diversity of Fauna:

The park is home to a wide variety of amazing animals that have adapted to life in the desert. Be mindful of the recognizable red kangaroos, wallabies, and shy echidnas. The vivid, spiky exterior of the Thorny Devil lizard enhances the allure of the desert.

2. A Birdwatcher's Paradise:

With over 170 different bird species, Uluru-Kata Tjuta is a birdwatcher's paradise. The striking mulga parrots and zebra finches add splashes of color to the landscape, and the majestic wedge-tailed eagle soars with grace. Pay attention to the captivating spinifex pigeons as they dart among the rocks.

3. Reptile Wonders:

The rocky peaks make for perfect habitats for reptiles. Observe the striking size and complex patterns of Perentie and Sand Goannas as they enjoy the sun. One of the poisonous residents, the Western Brown Snake, is evidence of the ecosystem's diversity in reptiles.

4. Nocturnal Marvels:

The wildlife gains a new dimension as the sun sets over the historic landscape. The animal kingdom comes to life at night in the Red Center. The enigmatic bilby, a marsupial that lives in the desert, forages beneath the stars while possums and bettongs come out of their daytime hiding places.

5. Conservation Efforts:

The present discourse aims to shed light on the continuous endeavors to maintain the intricate equilibrium of this distinct ecosystem. The mission of park rangers is to protect critically endangered species, like the rufous hare-wallaby, or Mala, and the Great Desert Skink. Examine the programs that emphasize the significance of conserving biodiversity in this dry setting.

6. Indigenous Views:
Learn how the Anangu people in the area perceive and interact with the wildlife. They have an intense understanding of the animals that inhabit this hallowed area as part of their profound connection to the land. Explore the Dreamtime tales from ancient times that have woven the origins of these creatures into the local mythology.

Nightlife

Uluru becomes a captivating canvas of stars as the sun sets, and its nightlife comes to life with distinctive experiences that combine contemporary entertainment with the historic grandeur of the Red Centre.

1. Stargazing Extravaganza:

As the day draws to a close, embark on guided stargazing tours that reveal the celestial treasures of the Southern Hemisphere. Take in the unobstructed view of the Milky Way, discover constellations, and listen to traditional Indigenous sky tales. It's a surreal experience that unites Uluru's natural wonders with the splendor of space above.

2. Sounds of the Desert:

Take in the sounds of the desert while attending outdoor events like concerts and performances. Uluru serves as a stunning backdrop for local musicians and Indigenous artists to display their skills, resulting in a tasteful blend of modern sounds and traditional rhythms. Listen to music that reflects the landscape and feel the pulse of Australia's red heart.

3. Under the Starlit Canopy:
Dine in style with a sumptuous dinner beneath the starry canopy for a more personal experience. A number of alfresco eating establishments combine delicious food with the peaceful ambience of the evening. Envision indulging in a thoughtfully prepared lunch beneath Uluru's gentle lunar glow, a silent observer.

4. Storytelling over a roaring campfire:

Join Indigenous storytellers as they offer engrossing tales. These stories explore the rich cultural past of the area, providing context for the Dreamtime and Uluru's significance. It's a private, immersive method of getting in touch with the land's spiritual essence.

5. Outback Bars and Lounges: Uluru's contemporary nightlife may be fully experienced in the outback pubs and lounges. With the iconic monolith as the backdrop, savor a variety of Australian wines, artisan beers, and creative cocktails. Uluru's antique charm and modern conveniences blend together in a perfect ambiance created by the gentle breeze, clinking glasses, and the calm murmur of conversations.

6. Night Tours & Walks:

Take guided night walks around Uluru's base to see how the rock changes in appearance when the moon shines on it. Learn about the nocturnal behaviors of local species, explore hidden caves, and feel the tranquil atmosphere of the desert at night. These trips offer a fresh viewpoint on Uluru's magnificence when bathed in the mellow glow of the moon.

7. Lunar Cinema Nights:
Immerse yourself in the wonder of outdoor cinema, where classic films and documentaries unfold against the backdrop of Uluru. This cinematic experience, complemented by the natural elements, provides an appealing blend of tale and the surrounding scenery.

8. Astrophotography classes:

Delve into the art of photographing the night sky with personalized astrophotography classes. Experienced instructors conduct hands-on teaching, assuring you depart with breathtaking views of the Milky Way arching over the hallowed locations.

Uluru's nightlife is a captivating blend of cultural immersion, natural beauty, and modern entertainment. It's a celebration of the ancient and the present, making every night in the Red Centre an experience to remember.

Chapter 9

Practical Tips for Traveling in Uluru-Kata Tjuta

Respect for Indigenous Culture

When visiting Uluru-Kata Tjuta, it is imperative to embrace the rich tapestry of Indigenous culture. Commence by recognizing the Anangu people, who have been the land's traditional stewards for thousands of years. Uluru is a place of tremendous spiritual significance; show respect by following traditional customs, which include not climbing it.

1. Cultural Awareness:

Be respectful when visiting Indigenous places. To gain a deeper grasp of the fascinating stories woven across the terrain, participate in cultural performances and guided excursions. Observe sacred spaces, which are designated by signage, and refrain from taking pictures in delicate regions.

2. Indigenous Art:

Take a deep dive into the colorful realm of Indigenous art. By acquiring genuine artworks and appreciating the tales they portray, you may help local artists. See the artistic traditions that have been passed down through the years directly by visiting art centers.

3. Language and Communication:

Communicating with Language:

As a show of goodwill, become conversant with a few simple Pitjantjatjara and Yankunytjatjara words. Appropriate communication shows respect for Indigenous history and creates genuine connections.

4. Guided Tours:
Choose guided trips with local guides. This helps you engage politely with the local population and gives you a greater appreciation of the sites' cultural value.

5. Tjukurpa
Get acquainted with Anangu legends, ancient law, and the idea of Tjukurpa. Your understanding of the culture will improve your enjoyment of the scenery and rock art.

Language And Useful Phrases

The ancestral occupants of this hallowed territory, the Anangu people, have a distinctive language and a rich cultural past. Although many people speak English, being familiar with the vocabulary of Pitjantjatjara (pronounced pi-jan-jah-jarra) and Yankunytjatjara (pronounced yan-kun-ja-jarra), the dialects of the Western Desert Language, can strengthen your ties to the region and its long-standing myths.

Start off with a brief greeting:
Palya:Hello/Good/Okay
Miri Nyuntu: How are you?
uwa (oo-ah) – yes
wiya (wee-ya) – no/don't

To show appreciation, use:
Minyma Ngalyuru: Thank you (said to a woman)

Tjamu Ngalyuru: Thank you (said to a man)

Numbers

Kutju (koo-joo) - 1

Kutjara (koo-djah-rah) - 2

Mankurpa (marn-koor-pah) - 3

Kutjara kutjara - 4

Kutjara mankurpa - 5

Ask about local legends, the past, and the environment:

Nganana ngurangka: What is this place?

Kanpinya nyangatja? Tell me a story.

Tjukurpa: Dreamtime stories

Ngura: Country/Place

When asked to eat with someone, show your gratitude by saying:

Nganana yumalunya: This food is delicious.

Become more connected with your environment:

Waru: fire

Kapi: water

Kuli: hot weather, summer

Wiru: beautiful

Pulka: big

Tjuta: many

Tjukula: rock

Nyinnga: frost

Wanari: wind

Pukulpa: happy

Tjitji (gee-gee) child

Ngun-tju (ngoon-choo) mother

Mama (mah-mah) father

If you're not sure how to pronounce a phrase, seek advice and repeat it with grace.

Safety and Health

It is important to carefully consider safety and health precautions when navigating Uluru-Kata Tjuta's striking terrain. A rewarding and safe journey is ensured by putting your well-being first, even in the face of unique challenges presented by the dry environment.

1. Being Ready for the Weather: Australia's desert climate can be quite harsh. Bring enough water with you when you go on adventures, and protect your skin from the strong sun by wearing sunscreen, hats, and sunglasses. Wear clothes that fit the weather. Pay attention to the heat, particularly during the hottest parts of the day.

2. Knowledge of Wildlife:

Experience the distinct flora and fauna sensibly. Avoid feeding wildlife and maintain a safe distance from them as well as respecting their habitats. It is in your safety and the preservation of the environment that you are aware of the local ecosystems.

3. Cultural Center Orientation:
For safety instructions, weather updates, and more information, start your visit at the Cultural Center. This makes you more aware of the circumstances and guarantees an informed exploration.

4. Emergency Contacts:
Make sure you are aware of the contacts and emergency protocols. Make sure you are aware of your surroundings and share your itinerary with others. Take along a

basic first aid kit, and be aware of the locations of local medical facilities.

5. Camping in a responsible manner: Observe the Leave No Trace guidelines when camping. Keep your environmental impact to a minimum, respect designated camping areas, and dispose of waste responsibly. By doing this, the special ecosystem will be preserved for upcoming generations.

6. Trail Etiquette:
To protect both yourself and other people, observe proper trail etiquette. If you're going on a longer hike, make sure you have enough water, a map, and the supplies you'll need. Also, let someone know about your plans.

You may guarantee your safety while visiting Uluru-Kata Tjuta and help preserve the rich cultural legacy that makes this location truly remarkable by implementing these helpful suggestions.

Shopping for Souvenirs

Discovering the lively markets in the vicinity of Uluru-Kata Tjuta presents a captivating chance to carry back concrete recollections from this age-old wonderland. With distinctive mementos that capture the essence of the Red Centre, you can fully immerse yourself in the rich culture and handicrafts of the nearby Indigenous communities.

1. Indigenous Artwork:
Explore the realm of Indigenous art, a rich manifestation of cultural heritage and

Dreamtime tales. Skilled local artists create exquisite paintings, dot works, and wood carvings that not only make for eye-catching mementos but also provide a significant link to the land's original owners.

2. Artisanal Jewelry:
Choose handcrafted jewelry that draws inspiration from the surrounding landscapes to adorn yourself with a piece of Uluru's essence. Every item tells a tale of the land's spiritual significance, from intricately designed pieces that showcase the vivid hues of the desert to those that feature sacred symbols.

3. Bush Tucker Treats:
Treat yourself to products infused with bush tucker and bring a little piece of the outback home with you. These culinary

delights, which range from exotic teas to native spices and jams, capture the essence of the area so you can continue to enjoy Uluru's flavor long after your visit.

4. Authentic Indigenous Fashion:
Invest in clothing with Indigenous design inspiration to update your wardrobe. You can take a little bit of Uluru with you everywhere you go when you wear clothing items decorated with traditional patterns and motifs. This creates a special fusion of style and cultural appreciation.

5. Local Handicrafts:
Browse the many handcrafted items available from the area, including didgeridoos, woven baskets, and pottery. These handcrafted treasures serve as useful and visually appealing mementos of your journey through the heart of Australia, in

addition to showcasing the artistic abilities of the local community.

6. Literature by Indigenous People: Invest in local authors' works to increase your knowledge of Aboriginal culture. You can delve deeper into Uluru-Kata Tjuta's cultural tapestry with these books, which range from Dreamtime stories to modern Indigenous literature. They offer profound insights into the history, spirituality, and connection to the land.

Custom Etiquettes in Uluru-Kata Tjuta

Understanding and honoring the traditions of the Anangu people, the original occupants of this hallowed place, is essential to embracing Uluru-Kata Tjuta's rich cultural legacy.

1. Acknowledging Traditional Owners
As you set out on your adventure, remember Uluru and Kata Tjuta hold special cultural significance for the Anangu, the land's original owners. Observe any boundaries in these regions and pay heed to the signage designating holy locations.

2. Photography and Videography
The scenery is stunning, but keep in mind that certain locations are sacrosanct and shouldn't be discussed or photographed. To maintain the cultural integrity of the place, always get permission before taking photos and be aware of any restrictions.

3. Quiet Reflection
Uluru is considered a sacred site, and it is traditional to observe quiet in specific locations out of respect. In order to respect

the land's sacredness, give yourself permission to simply soak in the energy of your surroundings without making needless noise.

4. Climbing Uluru

Although it was formerly permitted, climbing Uluru is now discouraged because of its cultural significance and security risks. Respect the Anangu people's wishes and opt for alternate, less invasive ways to take in the splendor of the rock, such base walks and helicopter excursions.

5. Exhibition of Culture

If you get to see traditional Indigenous acts, pay attention and show gratitude. No performance should be interrupted or recorded without authorization. Honor the storytellers and their performances, understanding the significance of preserving cultural information through these customs.

6. Honoring Tradition

It is important to understand cultural etiquette. It is usual to provide a cordial handshake upon first meeting someone. Recall to show respect towards seniors by respecting their experience and knowledge.

7. Gift-Giving

When giving gifts in situations when it is appropriate, make sure the things are considerate of other people's cultures. When ethically sourced local art and crafts are bought, they make heartfelt presents that benefit the neighborhood.

8. Move with care

Uluru-Kata Tjuta's delicate biosphere necessitates serious thought. To lessen your impact, stay on designated walkways, don't pick plants, and dispose of rubbish properly. You are helping to preserve this unique environment by walking carefully

9. Use Cultural Interpretation Centers to Your Advantage

To gain a deeper understanding of Uluru-Kata Tjuta's significance and history, visit the cultural interpretive centers. Using educational resources promotes sensitivity to and admiration for different cultures.

Traveling With Children To Uluru-Kata Tjuta

With your children, exploring Uluru-Kata Tjuta's breathtaking landscapes may be a fulfilling and enlightening experience. The following advice on traveling with kids in this magnificent red heart of Australia can help to ensure a smooth trip:

1. Family-Friendly Activities:
Take your kids on family-friendly excursions led by local tour guides to fully immerse them in the culture. Storytelling, art classes, and kid-friendly guided hikes are a few examples of these activities.

2. Safety Precautions:
Put your kids' safety first by packing sun protection items like hats, sunscreen, and reusable water bottles. Additionally, dress appropriately for the weather and pay attention to it.

3. Learning Opportunities:
Share the rich Indigenous history and stories connected to Uluru and Kata Tjuta to transform the trip into an educational

experience. Numerous educational insights provided by guided excursions attract the attention of young brains and establish a lasting connection to the country.

4. Interactive Exploration:
Inspire awe and interest in your kids by getting them involved in the process of discovering the surrounding natural marvels. Allow children to explore the distinctive rock formations and take in the colorful plants and animals that survive in this dry climate.

5. Sensitivity to cultural differences: instill in your kids the value of honoring Indigenous customs and cultures. This entails elucidating the importance of hallowed locations and motivating students to adopt an accepting and courteous attitude towards the native customs.

6. Feasible Accommodations: Opt for lodging options that are family-friendly and offer cozy, kid-friendly features. Play areas and swimming pools are among the amenities that many local resorts and campgrounds provide to keep the younger guests happy.

7. Flexible Itinerary
Give yourself permission to be spontaneous and to modify your schedule to fit your kids' interests and needs. Be willing to modify your plans in light of their preferences and energy levels.

8. Wildlife Encounters:
Make spotting animals for your kids an exciting activity. See wildlife such as wallabies, emus, and different species of birds. Seize the opportunity to preserve

these moments and the distinctive wildlife of the area.

9. The Enchanting Stargazing Experience:

Take your kids out to see the captivating Outback night sky. Choose a comfortable location and gaze up at the sky's wonders. In order to add a little magic to your family's evening, several lodgings also provide guided stargazing excursions.

10. Capture the Moments:

Take a picture with your camera or use your smartphone to record the unique times you spend with your kids in this amazing setting. These photos will be treasured recollections of a family trip in central Australia.

You and your kids will not only make the most of your time at Uluru-Kata Tjuta by using these suggestions into your family travel itinerary, but you'll also leave lasting memories behind. Take pleasure in the voyage through this amazing and hallowed territory!

Conclusion

Uluru-Kata Tjuta offers a voyage beyond typical travel experiences, as one is drawn into its mysterious landscapes and ancient wonders. The breathtaking Red Heart of Australia is explored in a riveting way by this Ultimate Guide, which unveils not only the jaw-dropping Uluru and Kata Tjuta rocks but also the rich tapestry of Indigenous stories woven into the very fabric of this sacred region.

Your guide will help you better comprehend Uluru's cultural significance as you go, revealing to you the close relationship between the Anangu people and the vivid red earth. Journeyers are invited to experience the throbbing stories of creation and spirituality that make up this holy site's rhythmic heartbeat.

The guide explores lesser-known gems that await the daring traveler in addition to the well-known sites. Encounters with the historic nature are personalized for tourists by means of obscure paths and secret nooks that reveal unforgettable experiences. Experience the timeless beauty of Uluru's ochre painting at sunrise and sunset with this tour that defies time.

The guide invites you to enjoy the seclusion of this ethereal setting as the sun sets, bestowing a warm glow across the untamed Kata Tjuta. Among the soaring domes, where the wind's whispers whisper the secrets of ages, it inspires reflection.

This guide is a kindred spirit in the heart of Australia's red centre, revealing the spiritual as well as the physical wonders that make Uluru-Kata Tjuta a soul-journey destination. This is a call to enter a world where the sound of rustling leaves carries old tales, and the vivid colors of the outback serve as a backdrop for treasured moments.

The Ultimate Uluru-Kata Tjuta Guide is more than just a manual for visitors exploring this sacred ground for the first time; it's a doorway to an eraless scenery and an introduction to the deep beauty that awaits those who answer its call.

Encouragement Quotes

Exploring new places is only one aspect of traveling; another is creating memories and having new experiences. Whenever you travel, bear it in mind. The following inspirational sayings could help you stay inspired while in Uluru-kata Tjuta:

"Travel makes one modest. You see what a tiny place you occupy in the world." - Gustave Flaubert

"Adventure may hurt you, but monotony will kill you." - Unknown

"The journey of a thousand miles begins with a single step." - Lao Tzu

"Traveling – it leaves you speechless, then turns you into a storyteller." - Ibn Battuta

The world is a book, and you only read a page when you do not travel - Saint Augustine

The experience of traveling "leaves you speechless and then transforms you into a storyteller." - A. Ibn Battuta

The journey, not the destination, is important. - T.S. Eliot

You can only purchase travel to increase your wealth. — Anonymous

Prejudice, intolerance, and narrow-mindedness die when they are exposed to travel - Mark Twain

"Exploration pays off." - Aesop

Useful Website and Resources:

1. Parks Australia - Uluru-Kata Tjuta National Park Website

Learn everything there is to know about Uluru and Kata Tjuta from the official source. This website is your go-to source for the most recent information, guided tours, park restrictions, and entry costs as well as cultural insights. Parks Australia: Kata Tjuta National Park at Uluru

2. Anangu Tours

Discover the essence of the native culture by traveling with Anangu Tours. In addition to sharing customs, legends, and the spiritual importance of Uluru and Kata Tjuta, they offer guided excursions. To have a genuine interaction with the old country, schedule a trip. Anangu Tours

3. Tourism Northern Territory

Tourism NT offers details on the surrounding places, lodging choices, and extra activities for a more comprehensive experience of the area. Discovering what the Northern Territory has to offer will improve your experience. Tourism Northern Territory

4. Australian Bureau of Meteorology - Uluru Weather

The Australian Bureau of Meteorology provides real-time updates so you can stay ahead of the weather. Make the most of your time in this magnificent setting by carefully planning your activities and consulting the weather. Uluru Weather

5. Uluru-Kata Tjuta Cultural Centre

The Uluru-Kata Tjuta Cultural Centre is a great place to immerse oneself in the area's rich cultural heritage. This resource center offers insightful information about the history, art, and ongoing preservation initiatives of indigenous peoples. Details about the Cultural Center

6. National Geographic - Uluru: Australia's Red Center

National Geographic's coverage on Uluru provides amazing photos and educational content for a virtual adventure and in-depth articles. Learn more about the cultural significance and geological wonders of the Red Centre. A feature of national geographic interest

7. Emergency Services - Northern Territory

Put safety first by being knowledgeable about emergency services. On its website, the Northern Territory Government makes sure you are aware of emergency contacts and protocols while you are there. Emergency Services NT

8. Uluru Camel Tours

Take a camel ride for a fresh viewpoint on the grandeur of the terrain. With Uluru Camel Tours, you can take an incredible trip across the desert and see the famous monolith's changing hues. Camel Tours of Uluru

9. Accommodation Choices on Booking.com:

Booking.com offers a selection of lodging choices. Find the ideal spot to relax after a day of exploring, from opulent resorts to affordable lodging options. For a hassle-free experience, Booking.com provides user reviews and simple booking alternatives.

10. Transportation Assistance with DriveNow:

You may compare and reserve rental vehicles there, and it makes traveling easy. Experience the freedom to explore Uluru and Kata Tjuta and the surrounding vast and stunning Australian landscapes at your own speed.

11. Interactive Map on Google Maps: Take advantage of the interactive capabilities of Google Maps to improve your trip planning. Determine the main areas of interest, hiking routes, and vantage spots surrounding Uluru and Kata Tjuta. By guiding you through the captivating scenery, our technology makes sure you make the most of your time there.

12. Photography Tips at Digital Photography School:

Digital Photography School offers photography tips that will help you capture the amazing splendor of Uluru and Kata Tjuta. Gain insightful advice and photographic strategies to improve your abilities and produce enduring memories of this breathtaking location.

Using these tools can help you make the most of your trip to Uluru-Kata Tjuta, combining natural beauty with a diverse culture to create a once-in-a-lifetime experience.

Printed in Great Britain
by Amazon